TODAY'S LESSONS
★ Social Studies - chap 9
★ Reading chap 10-12
★ English pg 30-35
★ Math pg 25-27
★ Science - test
★ Spelling lesson 7
★ Music

Mrs. Bearington
Room 103

©Teresa Kogut

Teacher, You Have Class!

artwork by Teresa Kogut

HARVEST HOUSE PUBLISHERS

EUGENE, OREGON

Teacher, You Have Class!

Text Copyright © 2005 by Harvest House Publishers
Eugene, Oregon 97402
www.harvesthousepublishers.com

ISBN 0-7369-1303-3

Original artwork © Teresa Kogut. Licensed by Linda McDonald, Inc., Charlotte, NC. It may not be copied or reproduced without permission. For more information regarding artwork featured in this book, please contact:

Linda McDonald, Inc.
5200 Park Rd., Suite 104
Charlotte, NC 28209
(704) 370-0057
www.lindamcdonald.com

Design and production by Koechel Peterson & Associates, Inc., Minneapolis, Minnesota

Harvest House Publishers has made every effort to trace the ownership of all poems and quotes. In the event of a question arising from the use of a poem or quote, we regret any error made and will be pleased to make the necessary correction in future editions of this book.

Printed in China

05 06 07 08 09 10 11 12 / LP / 10 9 8 7 6 5 4 3 2 1

Because you have class!

What office is there which involves more responsibility, which requires more qualifications, and which ought, therefore, to be more honorable, than that of teaching?

HARRIET MARTINEAU

Teaching is like gardening with knowledge being the water.

English
Science
Spelling
Math

Upon the subject of education, not presuming to dictate any plan or system respecting it, I can only say that I view it as the most important subject which we as a people may be engaged in.

ABRAHAM LINCOLN

❧⟡❧

I took the chalk and drew a large semi-circle in front of the board, drawing the chalk over such little feet as stood in the way, and when I told them to toe the chalk, there was such an eagerness to obey, that, for a minute or two, the whole class looked like a squad of adult recruits at their first drill. This movement attracted the attention of the rest of the pupils, and kept them still, so that the way was prepared for a lesson in the Alphabet.

WILLIAM B. FOWLE
Familiar Hints to Young Teachers

Aa Bb Cc Dd Ee

Order and method are so necessary in a school-room,
that there can be but few teachers who have not learned
their necessity, and how to secure their good effects.

N.W. Taylor Root

※～～

And when, for instance, I shall speak of soul,
Teaching the same to be but mortal, think
Thereby I'm speaking also of the mind—
Since both are one, a substance inter-joined.

Lucretius

※～～

Good teaching is more a giving
of right questions than
a giving of right answers.

Josef Albers

"Oh! I see now as plain as day; the cold air settles down all round, like the iron box, and drives up the hot air as fast as the fire heats it, in the middle, like the water; and so the hot air carries the smoke along up with it, just as feathers and things in a whirlwind. Well! I have found out what makes smoke go up—isn't it curious?"

"Done like a philosopher!" cried Bunker. "The thing is settled. I will grant that you are a teacher among a thousand. You can not only think yourself, but can teach others to think; so you may call the position yours as quick as you please."

WILLIAM HOLMES MCGUFFEY
McGuffey's Fifth Eclectic Reader

❧〜〜❧

You can't direct the wind
but you can adjust the sails.

AUTHOR UNKNOWN

A school-day was drawing to a close. In the classroom
the last lesson was in progress, peaceful and still. It was
elementary botany. The desks were littered with catkins,
hazel and willow, which the children had been sketching.
But the sky had come overdark, as the end of the afternoon
approached: there was scarcely light to draw any more.
Ursula stood in front of the class, leading the children
by questions to understand the structure and
the meaning of the catkins.

A heavy, copper-coloured beam of light came in at the west
window, gilding the outlines of the children's heads with
red gold, and falling on the wall opposite in a rich, ruddy
illumination. Ursula, however, was scarcely conscious of it.
She was busy, the end of the day was here, the work went
on as a peaceful tide that is at flood, hushed to retire.

This day had gone by like so many more, in an activity that
was like a trance. At the end there was a little haste, to finish
what was in hand. She was pressing the children with
questions, so that they should know all they were to know,
by the time the gong went. She stood in shadow in front of
the class, with catkins in her hand, and she leaned towards
the children, absorbed in the passion of instruction.

D.H. LAWRENCE

ONE NATION UNDER GOD

THE SPIRIT OF A TEACHER
IS THAT OF AN ANGEL

We think of the effective teachers we have had over the years with a sense of recognition, but those who have touched our humanity we remember with a deep sense of gratitude.

AUTHOR UNKNOWN

❦～❦

The job of an educator is to teach students to see the vitality in themselves.

JOSEPH CAMPBELL

❦～❦

Blessed are the hearts that can bend; they shall never be broken.

ALBERT CAMUS

❦～❦

What greater or better gift can we offer the republic than to teach and instruct our youth.

MARCUS T. CICERO

The important thing in life is
not the triumph but the struggle.

PIERRE DE COUBERTIN

❧⚬❧

The teacher should be familiar with at least
the outlines of mental science—the office of
each of the faculties of the mind, the order
in which they are naturally developed, and
the proper means of aiding in this development, so that the training and instruction
given may result in the most valuable of all
characteristics—a well-balanced mind.

HENRY KIDDLE
How to Teach

❧⚬❧

It is the supreme art of the teacher to awaken joy
in creative expression and knowledge.

ALBERT EINSTEIN

Anyone who stops learning is old,
whether at twenty or eighty.
Anyone who keeps learning stays young.

HENRY FORD

※———※

We left the classroom quietly, conscious that we
had been brushed by the wing of a great feeling,
though perhaps I alone knew Cleric intimately
enough to guess what that feeling was. In the
evening, as I sat staring at my book, the fervour
of his voice stirred through the quantities on the
page before me. I was wondering whether that
particular rocky strip of New England coast about
which he had so often told me was Cleric's patria.

WILLA CATHER
My Antonia

To teach is to learn twice.

JOSEPH JOUBERT

Be not angry that you cannot
make others as you wish them to be,
since you cannot make
yourself as you wish to be.

THOMAS À KEMPIS

Where there is an open mind
there will always be a frontier.

CHARLES F. KETTERING

Where there is an open mind
there will always be a frontier.

When asked what learning was
the most necessary, he said,
"Not to unlearn what you have learned!"

DIOGENES LAERTIUS

Learning is never done without errors and defeat.

VLADIMIR LENIN

❦━━❦

I have been maturing as a teacher.
New experiences bring new sensitivities and flexibility...

HOWARD LESTER

❦━━❦

The critical factor is not class size but rather
the nature of the teaching as it affects learning.

C.B. NEBLETTE

❦━━❦

Men learn while they teach.

LUCIUS A. SENECA

❦━━❦

Wonder is the desire for knowledge.

ST. THOMAS AQUINAS

The best way to know life is to love many things.

VINCENT VAN GOGH

Give me four years to teach the children
and the seed I have sown will never be uprooted.

VLADIMIR LENIN

Awaken people's curiosity. It is enough to open minds,
do not overload them. Put there just a spark.

ANATOLE FRANCE

There are two kinds of teachers: the kind that fill you
with so much quail shot that you can't move,
and the kind that just gives you a little prod
behind and you jump to the skies.

ROBERT FROST

❦──❦

In youth we learn; in age we understand.

MARIE VON EBNER-ESCHENBACH

❦──❦

Challenges make you discover things about yourself
that you never really knew. They're what make the
instrument stretch—what make you go beyond the norm.

CICELY TYSON

❦──❦

I touch the future—I teach.

CHRISTA MCAULIFFE

Find Beauty in a

It is in identifying yourself with the hopes, dreams, fears and longings of others that you may understand them and help them.

W.A. PETERSON

god's Creation

©Teresa Kogut

What sculpture is to a block of marble,
education is to a human soul.

JOSEPH ADDISON

Habits of punctuality and promptness are
of the utmost importance in school-teaching.

N.W. TAYLOR ROOT

❦

As a general rule, teachers teach more by
what they are than by what they say.

AUTHOR UNKNOWN

❦

The beginning is always today.

MARY WOLLSTONECRAFT

❦

Education...is a painful, continual and difficult work
to be done in kindness, by watching, by warning...
by praise, but above all—by example.

JOHN RUSKIN

Upon our children—
how they are taught—
rests the fate or fortune
of tomorrow's world.

B.C. FORBES

Success is the sum of small efforts—
repeated day in and day out.

ROBERT COLLIER

❧✦❧

Give the pupils something to do, not something to learn;
and the doing is of such a nature as to demand thinking;
learning naturally results.

JOHN DEWEY

❧✦❧

When we do the best that we can, we never know what
miracle is wrought in our life, or in the life of another.

HELEN KELLER

Teaching was the hardest work I had ever done,
and it remains the hardest work I have done to date.

ANN RICHARDS

❧━━━❧

If you want happiness for a lifetime, help someone else.

CHINESE PROVERB

❧━━━❧

Education makes people easy to lead, but difficult to drive;
easy to govern, but impossible to enslave.

HENRY PETER BROUGHAN

❧━━━❧

Develop a passion for learning. If you do,
you'll never cease to grow.

ANTHONY J. D'ANGELO

A teacher is one who makes himself
progressively unnecessary.

THOMAS CARRUTHERS

❧————❧

"Do you think you can maintain discipline?"
asked the Superintendent.
"Of course I can," replied Stuart. "I'll make the work
interesting and the discipline will take care of itself."

E.B. WHITE
Stuart Little

❧————❧

When teaching, light a fire, don't fill a bucket.

DAN SNOW

❧————❧

To waken interest and kindle enthusiasm
is the sure way to teach easily and successfully.

TYRON EDWARDS

If you treat an individual...as if he were
what he ought to be and could be, he will
become what he ought to be and could be.

JOHANN WOLFGANG VON GOETHE

❧❧

Teaching is leaving a vestige of one's self in the
development of another. And surely the student is a bank
where you can deposit your most precious treasures.

EUGENE P. BERTIN

❧❧

What the teacher is, is more important
than what he teaches.

KARL MENNINGER

The educator must above all understand
how to wait; to reckon all effects in the light
of the future, not of the present.

ELLEN KEY

❦

The entire object of true education is to make people
not merely do the right things, but enjoy them;
not merely industrious, but to love industry;
not merely learned, but to love knowledge;
not merely pure, but to love purity; not merely just,
but to hunger and thirst after justice.

JOHN RUSKIN

❦

The man who can make hard things
easy is the educator.

RALPH WALDO EMERSON

I PLEDGE ALLEGIANCE TO THE FLAG OF THE UNITED STATES OF AMERICA & TO THE REPUBLIC FOR WHICH IT STANDS ONE NATION UNDER GOD, INDIVISIBLE, WITH LIBERTY & JUSTICE FOR ALL.

© Teresa Kogut

I don't divide the world into the weak and
the strong, or the successes and the failures,
those who make it or those who don't. I divide
the world into learners and non-learners.

BENJAMIN BARBER

❧⤞~⤝❧

Take the attitude of a student;
never be too big to ask questions,
never know too much to learn something new.

OG MANDINO

❧⤞~⤝❧

Everyone who remembers his own
educational experience remembers teachers,
not methods and techniques.

SIDNEY HOOK

Education is not the piling on of learning, information, data, facts, skills, or abilities—that's training or instruction—but is rather a making visible what is hidden as a seed...To be educated, a person doesn't have to know much or be informed, but he or she does have to have been exposed vulnerably to the transformative events of an engaged human life... One of the greatest problems of our time is that many are schooled but few are educated.

THOMAS MOORE

❧~❧

Curiosity is the wick in the candle of learning.

WILLIAM ARTHUR WARD

No one has yet fully realized the wealth of
sympathy, kindness, and generosity hidden in
the soul of a child. The effort of every true
education should be to unlock that treasure.

EMMA GOLMAM

❧━━━❧

When love and skill work together,
expect a masterpiece.

JOHN RUSKIN

❧━━━❧

They may forget what you said,
but they will never forget how
you made them feel.

AUTHOR UNKNOWN

Kind words can be short and easy to speak,
but their echoes are endless.

MOTHER TERESA

It is not so much what is poured into the student,
but what is planted that really counts.

AUTHOR UNKNOWN

The teacher is one who makes two ideas grow
where only one grew before.

ELBERT HUBBARD

THE SPIRIT OF A TEACHER
IS THAT OF AN ANGEL

Man's mind, once stretched to a new idea,
never regains its original dimensions.

OLIVER WENDELL HOLMES

Never doubt that a small group of thoughtful,
committed individuals can change the world;
indeed it's the only thing that ever has.

MARGARET MEADE

Teaching is the greatest
act of optimism.

COLLEEN WILCOX